OF

Rum
COCKTAILS
David Biggs

Contents

INTRODUCTION

The word rum conjures up visions of swaying palm trees on white Caribbean beaches – a pirate ship may be gliding past in the distance. There's good reason for this romantic tropical image: rum is usually made from molasses, a by-product of the cane sugar-refining process. So rum is traditionally produced where cane sugar is grown, and that's in warmer, tropical climates like the West Indies, the Caribbean and Cuba.

Because of this connection, rum-based cocktails often include tropical fruit or fruit juices. Pineapples, bananas and limes play an important role. One of the exceptions (and also probably the best-known of all rum drinks) is the Cuba Libre, which goes back to 1893, shortly after Coca-Cola was developed. Apparently a Spanish army officer in Cuba added a splash of rum to the new soft drink and was very pleased with the result. Of course, no Cuba Libre is complete without a slice of cool lime. There's the tropical ingredient.

But rum's popularity goes back much further than that. It was issued to sailors serving in the Royal Navy as long ago as 1655. As with so many drinking traditions this one was based on sober common sense. On long voyages drinking water often became tainted, and beer certainly did not last long in ship-board conditions. Rum, however, could be stored for months in sturdy oak barrels. Mixed in equal parts with the ship's water, it killed any harmful microbes and improved the flavour enormously. This 50:50 rum–water mixture was named 'grog' after Admiral Vernon, known in the fleet as 'Old Grog' because he liked to wear a coat made of a rough material called Grogham.

It is interesting to note how many English expressions in use today have their roots in alcohol. Old sailors often suggest they 'splice the mainbrace' when they feel it's time for a drink. This comes from the days when sailors received a tot of warming alcohol before being sent aloft to repair the thick rope that controlled the large mainsail (and that only parted in particularly violent weather conditions). The unfortunates faced a hideously hazardous job trying to capture the flapping rope ends in gale-force conditions, bring them together and splice the frayed ends while clinging to the rigging for dear life. It needed an extra-large helping of Dutch courage to face up to that. When you were ordered to 'splice the mainbrace' your first reaction was to take a strong gulp of fortification; invariably this was ship's rum.

Stocking up

The three main rum categories are light (white rum), golden and dark. Commercially made light rum is often distilled in continuous stills and sold shortly afterwards, without maturation. The better dark rums are produced in old-fashioned copper pot-stills and aged for a considerable time in barrels before being bottled. For the serious cocktail maker it is probably sufficient to stock a light and a dark rum. Typical brands of light rum include Bacardi, Mainstay and Green Island. Dark rums include Myers's, Captain Morgan and Squadron. An interesting rum is Pussers, after the Royal Navy word for a purser, the officer who used to issue the daily rum ration. The producers claim a direct link to the original rum supplied to the naval ships.

Incidentally, the last official Royal Navy rum ration was issued on 31 July 1970, which became known as 'Black Tot Day'. Naval diehards around the world still mourn the occasion annually by raising a grog toast to a vanished tradition. Oh well, it's a good excuse for a drink, isn't it?

Equipment

It is worth investing in a few accessories that will make your preparations more enjoyable and enhance your reputation as a host. Equipment should

look and feel good, and do the job for which it is designed. Here's a short list of items the budding home bartender would need:

- sharp knife
- bottle opener
- ice bucket
- cocktail shaker
- ice tongs
- water pitcher
- measures (also known as 'jiggers' or 'tot measures'. It may be a good idea to have two measures, one being twice the capacity of the other.)

Glasses

Purists will be horrified if Planter's Punch is not served in a highball glass, or if Hot Buttered Rum is sipped from a lowball glass. Today things are more relaxed: if the drink fits in and it looks good – then so be it. There's a range of glasses available for rum cocktails, but you should get by with just four designs. A basic guideline is: the stronger the drink, the smaller the glass.

Cocktail glass   Lowball tumbler   Highball tumbler   Wine goble

- Cocktail – an elegant little glass with a shallow, flared bowl, and a stem to prevent your hand warming the chilled drink.
- Lowball – for drinks that have a large proportion of mixer to alcohol.
- Highball – intended for long drinks like fruit punches.
- Wine goblet – standard wine glass.

Decorating your Drinks

Cocktails should not only taste good, but smell and look good as well. And the tinkle of ice in the glass certainly sounds good.

Conscientious bartenders will ensure that all of their cocktails are a feast for the eye as well as the palate, but garnishes should never dominate. By adding just the right touch of garnish, you can give an indication of the flavour to be expected. A twist of lemon or lime tells the drinker to be prepared for a crisp, slightly tangy drink. A maraschino cherry on a cocktail stick, or a succulent ball of pink watermelon would indicate something sweet and syrupy. Some drinks are best sipped through a straw, and unless the glass is a tall one, a short straw is usually best. Trim off as much of a full-length straw as you require.

Many rum cocktails call for tropical fruit. Flavours may be enhanced by the addition of a slice of pineapple, a measure of lime juice, the addition of a tot of apricot brandy or a squirt of coconut milk. Appropriate fruits, when in season, can provide an exciting base. Bananas, melons, peaches and passionfruit can be liquidized in a blender to create a delicious fruit purée. Add rum to that and you have a superb drink.

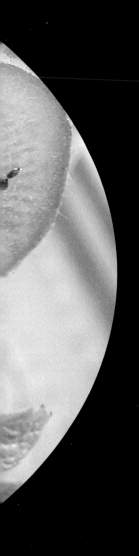

Classic
Collection

Brass Monkey

The 'brass monkey' in the name was the brass rack on which cannon balls were stored in the days of sailing ship warfare. In very cold weather the brass would contract and sometimes the cannon balls would no longer fit on the shrunken monkey and would pop out, causing some confusion as they rolled about on the gun deck. Hence the expression: 'Cold enough to freeze the balls off a brass monkey.' The cocktail is a good warmer when the temperature reaches brass monkey levels.

Ice cubes
One part light rum
One part vodka
Four parts orange juice
A slice of orange

- *Fill a highball glass with ice cubes and pour the rum, vodka and orange juice over them.*
- *Stir carefully and serve decorated with the slice of orange and a pretty straw.*

Daiquiri

Man is a creative animal and has been shown to adapt to almost any circumstances. American engineers working in Daiquiri, Cuba, were upset to discover they could not obtain their usual drink, bourbon, there. But there was rum in plentiful supply, so they set about creating a drink to replace their favourite tipple. The daiquiri was born. As with most famous cocktails, there are many versions of the daiquiri, but this simple one should serve as a starting point for the creative cocktail artist.

Ice cubes
One part light rum (traditionally Cuban, of course)
Juice of half a lime
Half a teaspoon of sugar
A slice of lime
A cocktail cherry

- *Place four or five ice cubes in a cocktail shaker.*
- *Add the rum, lime juice and sugar.*
- *Shake very thoroughly, then strain it into a cocktail glass.*
- *Decorate with a slice of lime and the cocktail cherry spiked on a stick.*

Cuba Libre

This classic cocktail is reputed to have been invented by an army officer in Cuba shortly after Coca-Cola was first produced back in the 1890s.

Crushed ice
One generous part light rum
Juice of a lime
Cola
A slice of lime

- *In a highball glass, place a small scoop of crushed ice and pour in the rum and lime juice.*
- *Top up with Cola and garnish with a thin wedge of fresh lime.*
- *It is usually served with a swizzle stick or stirrer.*

Rum Kiss

Nobody seems to know where this delicious cocktail originated, but it's great all the same.

Ice

One part Jamaica rum

One part Scotch whisky

A gentle splash of Pernod

A half teaspoon of lemon juice

A dash of maraschino bitters

A maraschino cherry

- *Shake the liquid ingredients well over ice.*
- *Strain into a chilled collins glass filled with crushed ice.*
- *Top with the cherry.*

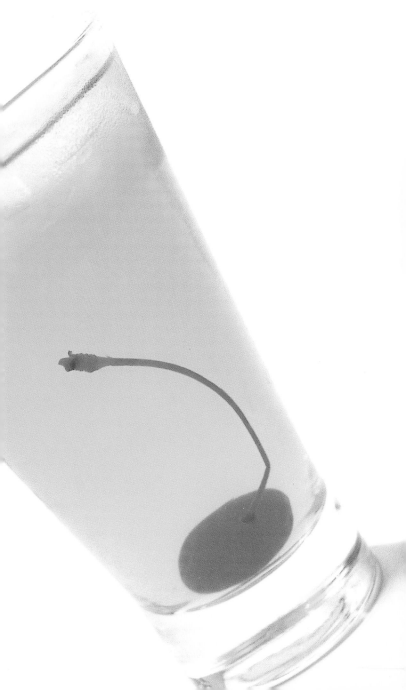

Mai Tai

Apparently the name of this classic comes from the Tahitan expression: *Mai Tai Roa Ae*, which means out of this world!

Ice

One part Curaçao.

One part apricot brandy

Four parts Jamaican rum

Juice of half a fresh lime

A splash of sugar syrup

A twist of lime peel

A chunk of pineapple and

A maraschino cherry

- *Shake the ingredients with ice in a cocktail shaker and strain into a chilled old-fashioned glass.*
- *Garnish with the pineapple, cherry and twist of lime peel. Out of this world!*

Long Island Iced Tea

In spite of its innocuous name, this drink packs enough clout to knock your socks off.

One part rum
One part tequila
One part vodka
One part gin
One part Triple Sec
One part lemon juice
A dash of sugar to taste
A generous splash of cola

- *Mix everything together except the cola, pour into a collins glass and gently add the cola, stirring just enough to mix it.*

Planter's Cocktail

There are several versions of this popular drink. Here's the simplest of them. You can make it into Planter's Punch by increasing the ingredients and adding a splash of Southern Comfort and a generous amount of soda water just before serving in a punch bowl.

Two parts light rum
One part lemon juice
One part of orange juice (optional)
Half a teaspoon of sugar

- *Shake well over ice and strain into a collins glass. (Or go the punch route.)*

Hot
Buttered
Rum

No collection of rum drinks would be complete without at least one recipe for hot buttered rum. It's a warm, sustaining drink to serve on a freezing winter's night by a roaring log fire. Buttered rum is mentioned by Charles Dickens in *Hard Times*. 'Take a glass of scalding rum and butter before you get into bed,' Bounderby says to Mrs Sparsit.

The peel of a lemon or orange
Whole cloves
One tablespoon of brown sugar
A cinnamon stick
Liberal helping of Jamaican rum
Half as much crème de cacao
A pat of unsalted butter
Grated nutmeg

- *Warm a large coffee mug by filling it with boiling water and letting it stand for a minute.*
- *While it is warming, take the citrus peel and stud it with as many whole cloves as you can.*
- *Empty the coffee mug and place the studded peel in it, together with the brown sugar and cinnamon stick.*
- *Add a little boiling water and stir until the sugar has dissolved.*
- *Now add the rum and crème de cacao and fill the mug with hot water.*
- *Remove the cinnamon stick.*
- *Drop in the butter, stir and sprinkle with grated nutmeg.*

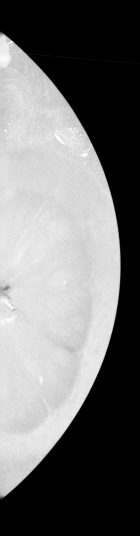

Island
Dreams

Banana Daiquiri

In his popular *Discworld* novels, author Terry Pratchett writes about an orang-utan who is inordinately fond of banana daiquiris. Readers all over the world send Pratchett recipes for this now-famous drink. This one is from a South African fan.

Two parts light rum
One part banana liqueur
One part fresh lime juice
Half a medium-sized banana
Crushed ice
A slice of kiwi fruit, if available

- *Place the rum, liqueur, lime juice and banana in a blender and blend for about 10 seconds until smooth and creamy.*
- *Add two generous scoops of crushed ice and blend for a further second or two, just to chill the drink.*
- *Strain it into a goblet, garnish it with the slice of kiwi fruit (or you could use a slice of banana in an emergency) and serve with a straw.*

Frozen Pineapple Daiquiri

Of course, you can go all the way with the tropical drink theme and make this rather exotic version of the famous drink. Looks good, tastes great!

One part light rum (naturally)
Juice of half a lime
Two teaspoons of Cointreau
Two slices of ripe pineapple, cut into cubes
Crushed ice
A cocktail cherry

- *Place the rum, lime juice, Cointreau and pineapple cubes in a blender and give them a whizz until the mixture is smooth and frothy.*
- *Half-fill a champagne flute with crushed ice and pour the mixture over it.*
- *Decorate with a final cube of pineapple and the cherry spiked together on a cocktail stick.*

El Burro

This delightful drink should be drunk in moderation if you don't want to make an ass of yourself!

Crushed ice
One part Kahlua
One and a half parts dark rum
One and a half parts coconut cream
Two parts thin cream
Half a banana
Sprig of fresh mint
Slices of banana

- *Place two spoonfuls of crushed ice in a blender and add all the other ingredients, except the mint and the slices of banana.*
- *Blend at high speed for about 10 seconds.*
- *Strain into a large goblet and garnish with the slices of banana and sprig of mint.*

Jolly Roger

Here is a lovely drink every pirate should know. It's quick and very easy to make.

Ice
One part dark Jamaica rum
One part banana liqueur
Two parts fresh lemon juice
A wedge of pineapple

- *Shake the liquid ingredients well over ice, strain into a wine goblet and garnish with the wedge of pineapple.*

Tahiti Club

Probably a firm favourite with the members of the Tahiti Club. Now it's there for everyone to enjoy. If you make the various parts large you can turn this into a superb summer cooler.

Four parts light rum
One part fresh lime juice
One part fresh lemon juice
One part pineapple juice
A slice of lemon

- *Shake the ingredients together with ice.*
- *Strain into a cocktail glass or a tall glass filled with crushed ice and garnish with the lemon.*

Henry Morgan's Grog

Grog was the name given to the mixture of equal parts of rum and water served to sailors in the British Royal Navy (as decreed by a naval officer nicknamed 'Old Grog' after the grogram jackets he liked to wear at sea). Captain Morgan's version of grog is rather different and far more powerful.

Crushed ice
One part dark Jamaican rum
Two parts Pernod
Two parts whisky
One part thick cream
Ground nutmeg

- *Place a scoop of crushed ice in a blender or cocktail shaker and add the rum, Pernod, whisky and cream.*
- *Blend or shake briskly until well mixed, and then strain it into a lowball glass.*
- *Dust ground nutmeg over it before serving.*

Jamaican Rhumba

Definitely a drink to put a bounce in your step.

Two parts of dark Jamaica rum
One part of Tia Maria
A couple of dashes of orange bitters
A tablespoon of fresh cream

- *There are two ways to serve this delight.*
- *Either shake all the ingredients together over ice and strain into a cocktail glass, or shake up everything except the cream, strain it into a collins glass and carefully float the cream on top.*
- *Two ways to terrific!*

Love
Potions

Shanghai Lady

We don't know who the original Shanghai Lady was, but her memory lingers on in this zesty drink.

Ice

Three parts golden rum

One part Sambuca

A generous dash of lemon juice

A dash of angostura bitters

A twist of orange zest

- *Shake the ingredients together with ice.*
- *Strain into a cocktail glass and decorate with the twist of orange zest.*

Lotus Land

Here's a very exciting little drink to start a romantic evening.

Ice
Two parts white rum
Juice of half a lime
One part raspberry liqueur
One part fresh cream

- *Shake all the ingredients vigorously with ice cubes and strain into a cocktail glass.*
- *You could add a maraschino cherry for decoration.*

Bolero
Cocktail

Like the famous music of this name, you may
become un-Ravelled after this.

Two parts light rum
One part Calvados (or cognac)
Juice of an orange
Juice of half a lime

- *Shake together well with ice.*
- *Strain and serve in a cocktail glass.*

Jade

This is a pretty green drink, as unusual to look at as it is to taste.

Three parts white rum
One part lime juice
One part triple sec
One part green crème de menthe
Sugar to taste
A slice of lime

- *Shake the ingredients together over ice, strain into a chilled cocktail glass and decorate with the slice of lime.*

Banana Bliss

Tropical fruit flavours all go well with rum to provide a good breath of Caribbean charisma to any party.

Two parts light rum

Two parts banana liqueur

One part fresh orange juice

A dash of Angostura bitters

A tablespoon of fresh cream

Sugar syrup to taste

Banana slices

- *Blend all the ingredients (except the banana slices).*
- *Strain into a collins glass and add the banana slices.*

Daiquiri Blossom

Not everybody enjoys the sharp astringency of the daiquiri described on page 12. Maybe it was fine for homesick mining engineers, but in the comfort of your own home or a cosy cocktail bar you may prefer this sweeter version. It certainly has a tropical flavour to it.

Ice cubes
One part light rum
One part freshly squeezed orange juice
A dash of maraschino
A slice of orange
A cocktail cherry

- *Place four or five ice cubes in a cocktail shaker. Add the rum, orange juice and dash of maraschino.*
- *Shake well and strain into a cocktail glass.*
- *Decorate with the slice of orange and the cherry speared together on a cocktail stick.*

Between the Sheets

The perfect end to a long day is to slip in between the sheets – crisp, clean and comforting. Perhaps the inventor of this cocktail felt all those attributes had been captured in the glass.

Ice cubes
One part light rum
One part brandy
One part Cointreau
A teaspoon of lemon juice
A twist of lemon rind

- *Place five or six ice cubes in a cocktail shaker.*
- *Add the rum, brandy, Cointreau and lemon juice.*
- *Shake well and strain into a cocktail glass.*
- *Serve garnished with a twist of lemon rind.*

Fluffy Duck

It's interesting how many of the cocktails containing cream are named after animals or birds. We have the burro, the pink squirrel and the grasshopper. Now meet the duck.

One part light rum
One part advocaat
Lemonade
Half a part thin cream
A fresh strawberry and a sprig of mint

- *Pour the rum and advocaat into a highball glass and fill almost to the top with well-chilled lemonade.*
- *Trickle the cream onto the surface over the back of a spoon and garnish with the strawberry and sprig of mint.*

Bee's Kiss

It's not hard to guess how this sweet delight got its name. As with any bee, however, too much familiarity could produce a sting.

Crushed ice

Two parts light rum

One part clear honey

One part thick cream

- *Place about a cup of crushed ice in a cocktail shaker and pour the rum, honey and cream over it.*
- *Shake vigorously until well blended.*
- *Strain into a chilled cocktail glass and serve ungarnished.*

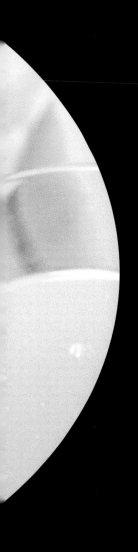

Festive Occasions

Havana Beach

This is a very quick and simple cocktail to make, but the results are always popular.

One part light rum
One part pineapple juice
A splash of lemon juice to taste
A sliver of fresh lime

- *Shake well over ice, strain into a cocktail glass and decorate with the sliver of lime.*

Corkscrew

This is a drink that could pop your cork.

Three parts light rum
One part dry vermouth
One part peach schnapps
A slice of lime

- *Shake the ingredients together with ice and strain into a cocktail glass, garnish with the lime slice.*

Zombie

A zombie is a corpse that has been brought back to life.
Maybe the name of this cocktail refers to its restorative
powers.

Ice cubes
One part dark rum
One part light rum
One part apricot brandy
One part fresh pineapple juice
A squeeze of lemon juice
A squeeze of orange juice
A slice of pineapple
A cherry to garnish

- *Place four ice cubes in a cocktail shaker and add the dark
  and light rum, brandy, pineapple juice and the two squeezes of
  citrus juice.*
- *Shake well and strain into a wine goblet.*
- *Garnish with a slice of pineapple and a cherry on a cocktail stick.*

Devil's Tail

Only the very brave can catch the devil by his tail, but those who do are safe from his horns. This is definitely a drink for the bold in spirit.

Crushed ice
Three parts light rum
One part vodka
One part apricot liqueur
One part lime juice
A dash of grenadine
Lime peel

- *Place a scoop of crushed ice in a shaker or blender and add the rum, vodka, apricot liqueur, lime juice (preferably fresh) and grenadine.*
- *Shake or blend well and strain into a lowball glass.*
- *Twist the lime peel over the glass and drop it into the drink.*

Xalapa Punch

This cocktail probably originated from Xalapa, a cathedral town situated in the province of Veracruz in Mexico.

Here again, the size of your measure will be determined by the size of your punch bowl. In these informal times almost any large bowl will do. I have even seen punch served in a brass-bound wooden bucket. It looked great!

The zest of two large oranges, grated
Two parts strong black tea
Honey or sugar to taste (about a cupful)
One part golden rum
One part Calvados
One part red wine
A block of ice
Orange and lemon slices

- *Place the grated orange zest in a saucepan and pour the hot tea over it to absorb the flavour.*
- *Leave it to cool and add the honey or sugar.*
- *Stir until dissolved.*
- *Add the rum, Calvados and red wine and place in the fridge to chill.*
- *When ready to serve, place the block of ice in the punch bowl, pour the punch over it and garnish it with slices of orange and lemon.*

Zombie Punch

There is something a little mysterious about the idea of a zombie, and this drink certainly has a murky and mysterious look to match its name. The flavour, however, is full of life.

Two parts light Puerto Rican rum
One part dark Jamaican rum
One part dark Demerara rum
One part Triple Sec
One part fresh lime juice
One part fresh orange juice
A quarter part lemon juice
A quarter part papaya juice
A quarter part pineapple juice
A splash of Pernod
A large chunk of ice
Pineapple slices

- *Mix all the liquid ingredients together in a large punch bowl, place the ice in the centre and allow it to stand for a few hours to chill.*
- *Before the guests arrive, taste it and adjust the flavour by adding the appropriate fruit juices or spirits.*
- *Garnish with slices of pineapple shortly before serving.*

Tom & Jerry

This classic cocktail is not actually named after the famous cartoon cat and mouse duo. It was invented way back in the 1850s by one Jerry Thomas, called 'The Professor', in his famous Planter's House bar in St Louis, Missouri. Later the name just naturally changed from Jerry Thomas to Tom and Jerry.

One egg
Half a part sugar syrup (or less to taste)
One part dark Jamaican rum
One part cognac
Boiling water
Grated nutmeg

- *Separate the yolk of the egg from the white and beat each separately.*
- *Fold them together and add the sugar syrup.*
- *Place this mixture in a warmed coffee mug, add the rum and cognac and top up with boiling water.*
- *Sprinkle grated nutmeg on top and serve piping hot.*

Apricot Pie

This is a fresh and appetizing little cocktail for summer drinking. It's tangy and fruity and absolutely guaranteed to have you coming back for more.

Crushed ice
One part light rum
One part sweet vermouth
One teaspoon apricot brandy or to taste
One teaspoon fresh lemon juice or to taste
One teaspoon grenadine or to taste
Orange peel to garnish

- *Place a generous scoop of crushed ice in a cocktail shaker or a blender and add the rum, sweet vermouth, apricot brandy, lemon juice and grenadine.*
- *Shake or blend well and strain into a chilled cocktail glass.*
- *Twist the orange peel over the drink to release the zest, then drop it in as decoration.*

First published in 2004
by New Holland Publishers
London • Cape Town
Sydney • Auckland
www.newhollandpublishers.com

86 Edgware Road, London,
W2 2EA, United Kingdom

80 McKenzie Street,
Cape Town, 8001, South Africa

14 Aquatic Drive, Frenchs Forest,
NSW 2086, Australia

218 Lake Road, Northcote,
Auckland, New Zealand

Publishing Managers
Claudia dos Santos & Simon Pooley
Commissioning Editor Alfred LeMaitre
Concept Design Geraldine Cupido
Designer Nathalie Scott
Editor Nicky Steenkamp
Stylist Justine Kiggen
Production Myrna Collins

Reproduction by
Resolution Colour Pty Ltd, Cape Town

Printed and bound in
Singapore by Tien Wah Press (Pte) Ltd

ISBN 1 84330 712 X

2 4 6 8 10 9 7 5 3 1